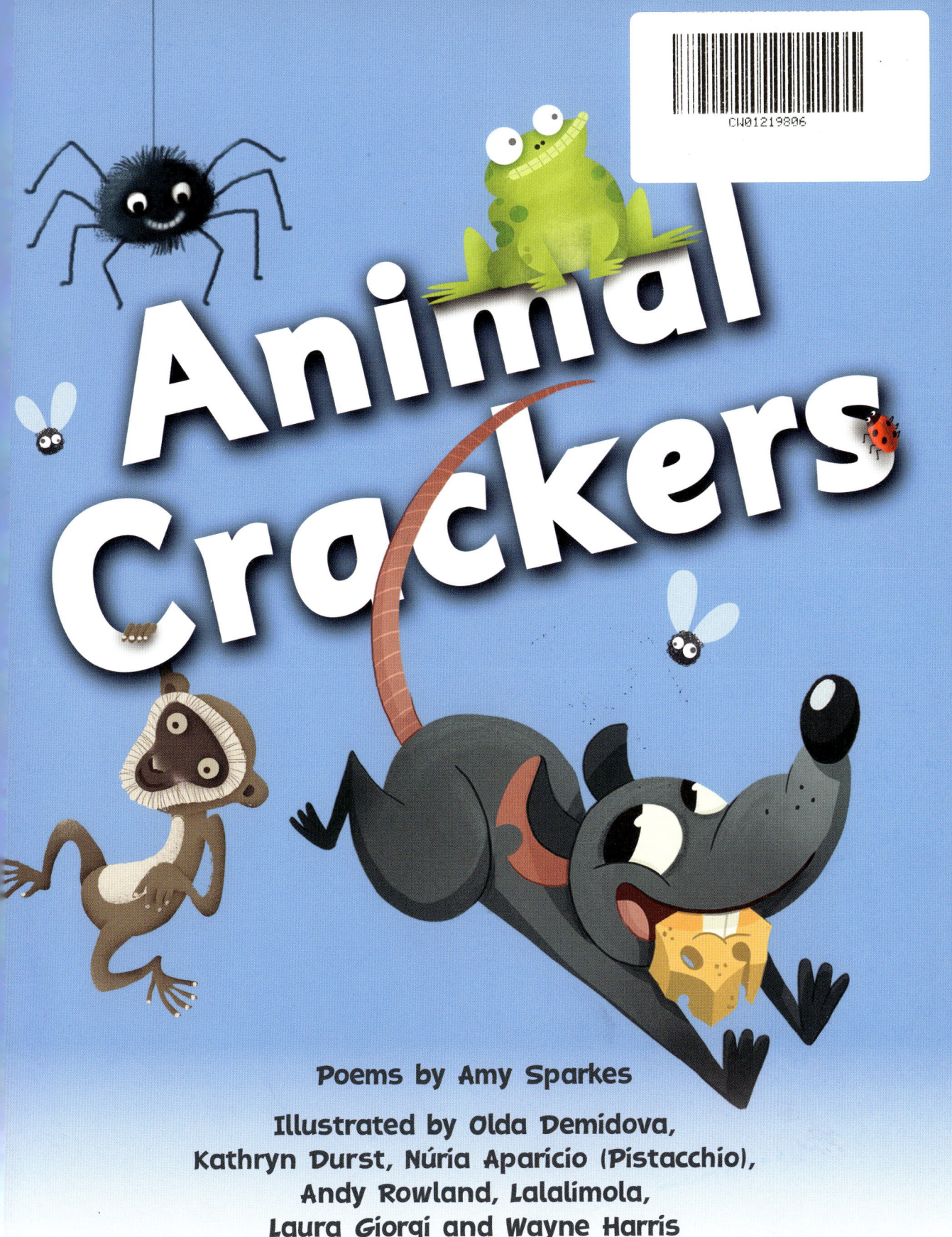

Animal Crackers

Poems by Amy Sparkes

Illustrated by Olda Demidova,
Kathryn Durst, Núria Aparicio (Pistacchio),
Andy Rowland, Lalalimola,
Laura Giorgi and Wayne Harris

Carl is a camel.
He has a hump that's lumpy.
Trotting down the road
It can get a bit bumpy!

Kangaroo

Kangaroo hops and hops.
Kangaroo never stops
Until he sees lollipops!
Then Kangaroo stops and shops.

Rat

Mum yelps, "Eek! A rat!"
Dad yells, "Get the cat!"

Cat runs, zooming past,
But Rat is just too fast!

Snail

There is Sid the snail,
He makes a silver trail.
From his shell he likes to peek.
He never wins at hide and seek!

Shannon is a shark.
She does not like the dark.
So when it's time for bed
She hugs Little Ted!

Zebra

Zak the zebra paints himself
In the animal park.
He forgot to check the tin –
Now he lights up in the dark!

Toad

Tess the toad must cross the road.
But cars keep passing by.
She starts to hop, then has to stop …